ITALIAN GARDENS.

ITALIAN GARDENS

·CHARLES·A·PLATT·

with

An Overview by Keith N. Morgan

and

Additional Plates by Charles A. Platt

A Ngaere Macray Book
SAGAPRESS/TIMBER PRESS
Portland, Oregon

An exhibition entitled
The Italian Garden Photographs of Charles A. Platt,
which includes the photographs from this book,
has been made possible
by the Art Program of the Bank of Boston.
Additional support was provided
by Paine Webber Group, Inc.
and The New York Botanical Garden.

The publishers would like to thank Charles A. Platt II
and other descendants of Charles A. Platt
for sharing the original glass negatives
from which the plates in this book were reproduced.

Frontispiece: Quirinal Gardens, Rome, arched entrance to the hedge walk.

Part I is reproduced from the original edition published in 1894 by Harper & Brothers.

ISBN 0-88192-273-0

Printed in Hong Kong

Sagapress, Inc./Timber Press, Inc.
9999 S.W. Wilshire, Suite 124
Portland, Oregon 97225

Library of Congress Cataloging-in-Publication Data

Platt, Charles A. (Charles Adams), 1861-1933.
  Italian gardens / by Charles A. Platt ; with an overview by Keith
N. Morgan and additional plates by Charles A. Platt.
      p.   cm.
  Originally published : New York : Harper, 1894.
  Includes bibliographical references and index.
  ISBN 0-88192-273-0
  1. Gardens--Italy. 2. Gardens, Italian. I. Morgan, Keith N.
II. Title.
SB466.I8P7   1993
712'.0945--dc20   92-33622
                                                        CIP

CONTENTS

LIST OF ILLUSTRATIONS

PART I

ITALIAN
GARDENS
by

·CHARLES·A·PLATT·

INTRODUCTORY

THE FIRST STEPS of one interested in the formal style of landscape architecture should be directed to Italy, where at the time
of the Renaissance the great gardens which have ever since
served as models of this method of design came into existence,
the form they took being the natural outgrowth of the architecture and art of the period. While the other arts of the Italian
Renaissance have been exhaustively treated in various forms
and languages, there is no existing work of any great latitude
treating the subject of gardens, the only one of importance
being that of Percier and Fontaine. This is an elaborate book by
two Frenchmen who studied the subject, and published, in the
early part of this century, a series of plates representing the
ground-plans and several views of each of the important Italian
villas. Their work was one largely of research and restoration,
the result of studying the history of the gardens and the existing
designs of their various architects. The outcome of such treatment is that their work fails to give a fair idea of the existing
state of the villas. The views from different points of the

A typical villa pavilion

gardens are so freely treated as to leave one familiar with them in much doubt as to their ever having looked as they are represented, and they are misleading, to say the least, to one who has never seen the gardens. The art of photography has been perfected since the treatment of the subject, and the object of the present writer has been by its means to illustrate, as far as possible, the existing state of the more important gardens in Italy, leaving out the matter of research altogether, since a more profitable study of the subject can be made as the result of these reproductions of nature, and it is quite possible (by making a careful study of all the gardens as a whole) to come to certain conclusions as to the fundamental principles which guided the original designers.

The gardens existing to-day have all passed through a variety of changes. Some of them have gone almost to ruin through neglect or difference of taste in their owners, and, with one or two exceptions, those which are at present the most carefully kept up have suffered the most severely from the changing fashion of the time. However, in almost all of them there is something of their best time which, either by reason of the great difficulty of alteration or from some other cause, has been allowed to remain. It has been attempted in the illustrations here given to reproduce these traits and such others as seem good in themselves.

It should be said here that the word "villa" is used in the Italian sense, implying all the formal parts of the grounds arranged in direct relation to the house, the house itself being as much a part of it as the garden or the grove.

The evident harmony of arrangement between the house and surrounding landscape is what first strikes one in Italian landscape architecture—the design as a whole, including gardens, terraces, groves, and their necessary surroundings and embellishments, it being clear that no one of these component

Terrace casino of an Italian garden

parts was ever considered independently, the architect of the house being also the architect of the garden and the rest of the villa. The problem being to take a piece of land and make it habitable, the architect proceeded with the idea that not only was the house to be lived in, but that one still wished to be at home while out-of-doors; so the garden was designed as another apartment, the terraces and groves still others, where one might walk about and find a place suitable to the hour of the day and feeling of the moment, and still be in that sacred portion of the globe dedicated to one's self.

Old print of an Italian garden

:VILLA:LANTE:

THE MOST COMPLETE example of the Italian villa—that is, the one best preserving its original form—is the Villa Lante, at Bagnaia, not far from Viterbo. This, like all the great villas, was the work of several designers carried through the lives of several owners, but the most important part was from the designs of Vignola, and sufficiently completed in his lifetime to give his stamp to the whole. While a considerable part of the park has been allowed to go to decay, the house and gardens and all that part of the design known as the "villa" have been kept up, and probably to-day present a better idea of the Renaissance garden than does any other in Italy.

The flower-garden of the Villa Lante is southwest from the house, or rather houses, there being two, one for domestic purposes and the other for entertainments. These are at either end of the terrace which overlooks the garden. The principal street of the town leads directly up to the gate, upon entering which one finds one's self in the midst of a profusion of flowers, and facing a fountain which makes the central feature of the garden.

Fountain and flower-garden, Villa Lante

The fountain consists of a group of bronze figures on a circular base surrounded by four large basins, which receive the falling water. Looking beyond the fountain, the eye is led, by means of a series of terraces and fountains between the two houses, to the highest part of the land; this is thickly covered with trees, which form a background for the architectural features. The garden proper covers about an acre of ground, but so large a space is taken up by the fountain and its surrounding embellishments that the actual space for planting is much less than one would imagine. A magnificent box hedge, very dense and high,

Fountain of the Moors, Villa Lante

protects the garden on the north and west, the south being open and overlooking the extensive campagna. Making a part of the eastern wall is the orangery—a building which forms a very necessary part of every garden in Italy—wherein the orange-trees and the tender plants grown in pots are stored in winter. The important paths of the "parterre" are marked by small box hedges, accented at the corners by large orange-trees in pots.

The main features of the garden are so admirably arranged that there is no point of view from which the effect is not good. The problem of treating so large a space was rendered difficult from the fact that the chief point of view is from the house terrace, necessitating a large scale in the architectural details and in the cut forms in green. The large lines of ponds surrounding the fountain form the basis of the scale, the large stone vases at the corners being balanced by forms of corresponding size on the surrounding paths. These large forms are filled in on the architectural part with balustrades and small carving, and among the growing things the flowers and small plants. Thus from above the four sheets of water reflecting the sky form the necessary contrast to the various characters of the planting and the formal details.

Two stone staircases lead to the terrace which connects the houses. Another fountain marks the centre of this terrace, and the whole is shaded by large sycamore-trees; and here, between the garden and the wood, the family live. If they wish sunshine, they turn one way; and if cool and shade and the sound of running water, the other; though, for that matter there is no place in the villa where the trickling of a fountain may not be heard. Another series of staircases, combined with fountains, leads up from this terrace to a walk on either side of the watercourse, conducting the water from the upper fountains to those we have just passed. At the top is the "bosquet" or grove, and in its centre, flanked by two most beautiful pavilions, is the reservoir. This is, in its turn, enclosed in a kind of court of Doric columns, supported on pedestals and connected by balustrades.

The sylvan court thus composed makes the bosquet of the Villa Lante one of unusual beauty. The trees behind the columns form a dense glade. The branches of the trees are alllowed to grow in and out, making the effect that of being surrounded by a forest. The two pavilions which mark the corners of this enclosure deserve special attention; there is nothing of the kind in any other villa, and they form the key-note of an

Casino stairway, Villa Lante

Pavilion, Villa Lante

exceedingly well-conceived place.

It will be seen that in the Villa Lante the main features of the Italian villa are found in much of their original perfection—namely the house, the flower-garden, the terrace, the grove, the fountains, and the water system; and a general study of other villas will show that their different dispositions are the result of harmoniously combining these different parts with the natural formation of the land. If any prominence is given to one or the other of these features, it is suggested by some natural cause. The Villa Lante is built on gently rising ground, and there is less terracing here than in the sites usually selected for Italian villas. In no other, however, are there so many important characteristics still to be found. Moreover, the arrangement is so compact, and the relation of one part to another is so obvious, that they seem to justify its selection as the starting-point in the study of Italian gardening; not because it is the most important or the most beautiful, but because it serves best as a key by the aid of which one can go to the less perfect villas and better understand their probable arrangement.

In the garden, Villa Lante

VILLA·BORGHESE

IN ROME the most important villa, on account of its size, is the Borghese; but here very little now remains beyond the main forms of the original plan. Especially that *intime* portion of the gardens immediately surrounding the house has been allowed to go to decay. There is no large flower-garden making a feature in itself, though at the time the villa was kept up a great many flowers were grown throughout the place, and there were several small flower-gardens of minor importance. There were two of these of especial interest, one at either end of the casino; but nothing now remains of them but the high walls by which they were enclosed, and some traces of the fountains. Beyond the fine avenue and walks, the one feature of interest in the Borghese at present is the Piazza di Siena—the old race-course—and how much of this may be the result of change it is difficult to know. It is, however, so delightful now that one does not care to be too curious about its past. Its shape is oblong, the sides gently terraced by stone steps (now greatly overgrown with grass), and at the end are a fountain and a magnificent walk of old ilex-trees. On the two long sides, behind the steps, are rows of very fine stone-pines. In early summer this is a favorite resort of the people, who come to sit on these grassy steps and to walk about on the lawn. Although there are no races, I have seen quite enough of a gathering here to give an idea of its ancient look on a gala-day. No more charming theatre for an outdoor entertainment, either equestrian or athletic, could possibly be imagined.

There are many architectural details of interest in the Villa Borghese, some fine gates and fountains and stone benches. These are most all seemingly detached now, but once formed a part of the elaborate plan of the villa. One of the most interesting features is the wall enclosing the open space in front of the casino. This is most skilfully designed for the gentle slope of the land, stone benches alternating with balustrades. It is very suggestive as an admirable enclosure for a terraced garden. There is much that is suggestive in the detached garden architecture of the Italian villas, their surroundings are so often in bad taste and their original meaning quite lost sight of.

Piazza di Siena, Villa Borghese

VILLA·PAMFILI

OF THE VILLA PAMFILI the flower-garden is all that has kept its original form, and here the details of the arrangement of the "parterre" have been quite changed, and are now very much too hard and cut up. The disposition of the house in relation to the garden is somewhat similar to that at Lante, the house making a part of the terrace which overlooks it, the difference being that there is here but one house facing the centre of the garden, instead of one at either end. The garden occupies an enormous space at the south of the house, its west end being cut out of the side of a hill and walled in, and its east end forming a terrace. To see this garden to advantage one should be either in it or in the house, as from a distance the boxlike form of the building offends one's sense of proportion. The original scheme of the architect was never carried out, if we are to believe an old print, which adds two long wings to the house, and gives, in connection with it, an admirable arangement of trees, which would have vastly improved the general effect. What remain of the old garden are its fine proportions, the

Flower-garden, Villa Pamfili

walls and gates at the west, and the beautiful staircases and balustrades at the south and east. The central fountain has been removed, and the only water there now is in the basin at the enclosed end. The arrangement of the flower-beds is made up of scroll-work in box or gravel, but there are no fine large forms, such as should surround this smaller work. The result is that the paths are everywhere too obvious, and the hardness of the design offends one at every turn.

This lack of harmony is made particularly manifest by a very beautiful circular form given to the western terrace. There is no approach to this from below, and its position in a mass of irregularly placed trees with grass growing about its base is particularly unfortunate, and gives it a very detached look. There is a large plantation of stone-pines in the more remote parts of the villa. These were placed there by the great French landscape architect, Le Nôtre. They give a certain dignity to the drives and from a distance suggest a more interesting place than one finds upon closer examination.

There is a fine avenue of ilexes at the west end of the garden; and there was once, at the south, an elaborate system of hedges, plantations, and architecture leading the eye off into the distance. This has now all been done over in the English manner, with irregular clumps of trees, and wide stretches of lawn, quite out of harmony with the formal plan of the villa. The south wall is typical of what a garden wall should be— covered as it is with vines of every sort. These make masses of varied greens, which, with the bloom of the flowers is very telling against the white wall.

Bird's-eye view, Villa Pamfili

33

VILLA ALBANI

THE VILLA ALBANI was made at the end of the eighteenth century, and consequently the architecture is very florid in character. Though the general plan is a good one, the prominence given to the architecture makes the effect of the whole hard, and particularly so on account of the paucity of the planting. The flower-garden has no flowers in it! or such, at least, is its effect. The garden is so placed—being sunk between the house and a pavilion which encloses its end—that it is impossible not to look down upon it. This is the usual placing of Italian flower-gardens; but to look well under these conditions very full planting is absolutely necessary. Here one looks down and sees nothing but scroll-work in box, and great varieties of colors in gravel and sand occupying spaces that should be filled with flowers, all the efforts of the gardener going to make a permanent effect and to preserve his design at any cost, the result being the reverse of that looked for in a flower-garden, the design, indeed, being made altogether unpleasant by its hardness. The other features of the Villa Albani have not suffered as the garden has, and the ilex walk leading from the south wing of the house is unusually fine, being slightly elevated above the house, and approached by a handsome flight of steps. In this walk there are some very interesting statuary and old Roman tables. The cypress hedges at the south of the garden are as fine as anything in Italy. They are admirably arranged with columns at intervals; these, with statuary, make a fine contrast by means of their deep green background. The entrance to the villa is somewhat weak, but it leads to an interesting circle of stone-pines surrounding a high column. The weakness lies in the fact that one's eye is not led beyond this, and that there is no evident avenue of approach to the house.

The interest in the plan of the Villa Albani lies in the fact that the ground it covers is very nearly flat, the garden alone being lower than the rest of the villa. The architect had none of the advantages of a site naturally interesting in itself, and no natural formation in the landscape to suggest treatment, so that the design is specially worthy of study as a pure creation.

QUIRINAL GARDENS

THE ROYAL GARDENS are an interesting study on account of the great height of the hedge growth. Judging from an old print of the plan of this garden, it was originally laid out in a very open manner as an enormous "parterre." There is but one level throughout the plantation, and this was cut up into large squares surrounded by low hedges enclosing flowers. The fountains and statuary were very frequent, and at the sides the walks were shaded by ilex-trees. The great height of the hedges which once marked the borders of the beds have now turned these enclosures into most charming apartments, the passages from one to another being arches cut through the dense growth. In some places the hedges of laurel, box, and ilex reach a height of thirty feet, and as a growth in itself is remarkable; but when one finds it formed into courts connected by long alleys, and with the doorways and arches apparently carved in the dense green, the effect is quite wonderful. There is nothing at all like it in any of the other gardens; it is quite unique. To one who doubts the advantage of straight lines in gardening, the extreme beauty of the perspective in the Quirinal would teach much. The principal hedge walk nearest the palace shows this at its best. At the right of the path is the great ridge leading in a perfectly straight line to the limit of the garden; on the left are formal beds filled with flowers, allowed to grow much as they will, and the formality of the mass cut up by trees and flowering shrubs. Pots of azalias and orange-trees are placed here and there to make the opening of the smaller paths, near to sides of the wall, form a contrast one to another, and make of the whole a most complete and satisfying garden effect. There are other parts of the garden that have not been so skilfully treated, and where the admirable opportunities, the result of time and overgrowth, have been neglected. An attempt to produce an English lawn is misplaced here, and the disposition of the statuary and the surroundings of the fountains are unfortunate. These things are lost sight of, however, in the beauty of the greater part of the garden, the charm of the old walks, and the delightful seclusion of the green walled courts.

An overgrown corner, Quirinal Gardens

COLONNA GARDENS

FOR A FLOWER-GARDEN, pure and simple, there is none more charming in Italy than the Colonna. In the very heart of Rome, it is so concealed that one might pass it a hundred times without suspecting its existence. The palace is at the foot of a hill, and is separated from the garden by a sunken street and terraces. The street is crossed by several bridges, and in looking from the palace to the terraces is entirely invisible.

The hill is very abrupt, and one is led through ilex walks and up stairways, along terraces, to the flower garden at its very top. The garden, however, is not in so unsheltered a position as this might seem to indicate, being protected at the south by a high hedge. An iron gateway at an opening in this hedge forms the entrance to the garden, and on passing through this, one is immediately in the midst of a most beautiful mass of bloom, where all growing things seem at their best. The arrangement of the garden is very simple, the paths all radiating, like the spokes of a wheel, from a central basin. The beds are slightly elevated above the walks, and their borders of box form the borders of the paths; the area covered is about half an acre, but so admirable is the plan and so compact the planting that it seems much larger, one sees no paths except that upon which he is standing, seeming always to be surrounded by a great profusion of flowers, with just enough of formality to give them their value.

There is no architectural feature in this garden beyond the basin in its centre, which is sufficiently low to receive the reflection of the growth about it. The garden owes its charm—which is very great—to its very simple design and the admirable planting. It is enclosed on the east and west by high

The Colonna flower-garden

42

Cypresses, Colonna Gardens

walls covered with vines; at their basis are several tiers of steps with flower-pots.

The Colonna, for its size, is by no means important in comparison with others of the well-known gardens, but it is most instructive in its simplicity and charm when contrasted with such gardens as Albani and Pamfili, where everything has been lost sight of but the preservation of an elaborate "parterre." The flower-garden of this villa is so distinctively itself an interesting feature that it is unnecessary to dwell much upon the rest; though the lower terrace, on a level with the first floor of the palace, is also something of a garden, and interesting in itself. It is planted in long tiers, with flowering shrubs bordered by tree-roses, and terminating at the west in a grotto with columns and tall cypresses, and at the east in old statuary half covered with vines and undergrowth.

The side-hill between this and the upper garden was originally occupied by old Roman baths, and the architect has, wherever possible, allowed the mason-work to remain, sometimes forming the old arches into stairways or terraces, and leaving the old brick walls to be covered with vines.

VILLA MEDICI

THE VILLA MEDICI, now the property of the French Government, has the most delightful situation in Rome—east of the gardens of Pincio and slightly elevated above them. The entrance to the garden is by a roadway at the left of the villa, and leads immediately into a beautiful grove with straight paths and fountains. Considering its position, this seems really a forest, and one has something of a stroll before reaching the old flower-garden behind the villa. Here most of the traces of the flowers and their original arrangement have disappeared, and little is done to keep the place up in its old glory; even the main features of the "parterre" have been changed with a view to economy, and only the general effects produced by the situation and its relations to the other parts of the villa are left.

There is, however, a great charm in the sharp-cut box hedges which surround the flower-beds, in contrast with the varied outlines of the grove through which we have just passed. These hedges are so high that one misses the flowers as little as possible, although of course they lead one to pass through the garden, rather than to treat it as a place in which to loiter.

Above the flower garden, to the east, is an architectural terrace leading to an ilex bosquet. This is really the charming feature of the Villa Medici to-day, and there is nothing more delightful in Rome. The trees are very old, and although the place is not large, there is such a complete tangled growth that it is impossible to believe that one is within a stone's-throw of a very busy part of the city. At the end of the central paths is an elevated temple, reached by a flight of steps, and the trees surrounding it are so cut as to give a complete view of the city. There are some delightful old seats in the grove, which one abandons with regret when the custodian arrives to close the gates and turn the visitor away.

The box walk, Villa Medici

VILLA MATTEI

ALTHOUGH this was once one of the most magnificent gardens of Rome, there is very little there at present to suggest this. The interest that one finds is rather in the study of the ancient place than in the beauty of the existing landscape architecture.

The villa has been through a period of great ruin, and the style of gardening in vogue at the time of its partial restoration was quite the opposite of that upon which it was originally designed. The result has been to give its general appearance one without character as a complete work of art, the contrast between the formal and the so-called neutral methods filling one with a sense of lost opportunity. The main features of the old work were of such magnitude as to be ever before the eye, showing what might have been or what has been. The more recent work has been chiefly an attempt to conceal this, or to cover the evidences of its ruin. Although the effect of the villa is thus as a whole so unsatisfactory, there are parts, taken by themselves, full of charm, and among these are a series of alleys leading from a small central fountain. High hedges border the

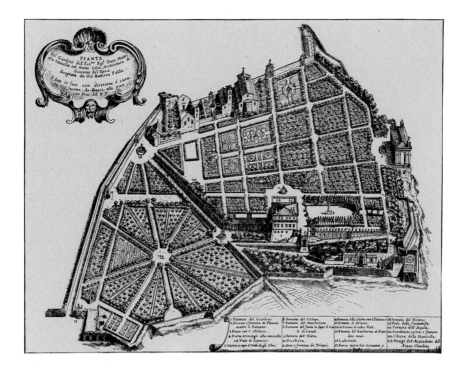

Plan of Villa Mattei

paths, and behind them are tall stone-pines, giving shade and marking the perspective of each of these walks as the eye follows them to the end. The flower-garden, though not intended as a show feature, is very interesting in its simplicity. It is intended simply as a place to grow flowers for cutting, and an absence of any design not necessary for the convenience of the gardener has given the place a quaint character which one rarely finds as a result of design. In the centre is a basin from which the flowers are watered, and the beds are in long lines, with a wide path only in the middle of the garden, the lateral ones being lost by the growth of the plants. There are many bits of statuary and architectural details of the Roman time, once used to decorate the gardens of the Villa Mattei. These are now placed often where they do not add to the general effect, but at least where they may be studied by the archæological student.

48

An old alley, Villa Mattei

VILLA D'ESTE

IN TURNING from the gardens of Rome and its immediate environs, the Villa d'Este, at Tivoli, is the most important, and, in fact, if one could study but a single villa in Italy, this should be the chosen one.

In its day it was undoubtedly the finest villa in Italy, and although it is now in a state of great dilapidation and decay, its natural advantages and the great beauty of its situation are such, and the construction of its main features so admirable, that it still remains a noble example of landscape architecture of the Renaissance. Not nearly so large as the Borghese or the Pamfili Villa, every inch of its ground has been utilized to the utmost, and the whole arrangement is compact and complete.

The site of the palace is at the top of an abrupt hill-side, overlooking the campagna, and the architect's problem lay in the treatment of the extremely abrupt slope, there being no natural flat space except at the bottom of the enclosure, which is still high above the surrounding country.

The palace itself is built on terraces, the court and entrance

View from top of porch, Villa d'Este

being three stories higher than the first open terrace in front of the house. Beyond these a most elaborate system of terraces, connected by stairways and fountains, brings one down to the large terrace below. Beyond the magnificent site, the greatest natural advantage of the place is a practically unlimited supply of water. This the architect has used in every conceivable way, and in addition to the great variety of fountains and grottos there is hardly an architectural feature in the villa in which a play of water is not made to form a part. It might be added that they are now to be found in almost every imaginable state of decay. Most of the fountains and other architectural features have long since been stripped of their finest pieces of statuary, and in being thus stripped many of them have lost their *raison d'être.*

The excavations of Hadrian's villa are the mine from which they were originally taken, and they have now, most of them, found their places in museums, being too valuable to be left in a spot so long uninhabited.

The palace is an enormous structure of perfect simplicity of design, its long lines contrasting with the elaborate terraces which support it. The only decoration of its exterior is the doorway and staircases leading to it. This is connected with the rest of the garden by the chief system of fountains and staircases, which lead the eye from the lower terrace to the house. To one looking up from below, the intricate design of this doorway appears like most delicate lace-work in comparison with the extreme simplicity of the otherwise unbroken façade of the house, and in contrast with the deep green of the terrace plantation. Looking down from the upper terrace, one sees through a deep cut in the foliage, over a series of fountains and stairways, the large circular fountain on the lower terrace, surrounded by gigantic cypresses, and beyond this the immense expanse of the campagna.

There are many cypresses throughout the planting which have now grown to an enormous size. These, with their hard-cut edges and sculpturesque forms and great depth of color, make a wonderful foreground for the infinitely increasing delicacy of the campagna as it loses itself in the sky at the horizon.

There is no flower-garden now at the Villa d'Este, and such is the overgrowth of hedge plants and shrubs on the lower terrace that one would hardly suspect that here was once an elaborate "parterre." At present one finds no flowers at all, except those which have grown wild, and these are frequently

In the gardens, Villa d'Este

to be found where there should be none. In an arrangement so varied as that at D'Este any opportunity for simplicity was valuable, and one was found in the ponds or canals at the foot of the first line of terraces. The form here is perfectly simple, in long straight lines surrounded by high hedges, now overgrown almost into small forests. These ponds are now comparatively stagnant; but they were originally filled by many jets of water flowing from the vases which marked their borders. At present, of course, only the general form is left, and though that is still fine, the great overgrowth of the surrounding hedges naturally dwarfs their effect, and the stairs above them are quite concealed. The old stairway of the Condonata, which was bordered by fountains from top to bottom, is now too overgrown to be seen, and this is the case with many beautiful parts of the villa. While this wildness has given a certain charm of its own to the place, it makes it difficult, if not impossible, to trace much of the original design of the architect.

Many of the architectural features have been restored at unfortunate periods or by unskilful hands, and are now far from being in harmony with the simplicity of the earliest work of the villa. It is where the overgrowth has concealed this sort of thing that time has done so much in making the present charm of the villa.

VILLA·ALDOBRANDINI·

AT ABOUT the same distance from Rome as Tivoli, and with very much the same situation and character of country (except that it is less abrupt), is Frascati, which contains a very remarkable collection of villas. Though none of them were so elaborately conceived or so perfectly carried out as the Villa d'Este, and though in their present condition there is no individual villa of any striking importance, yet, taking the place as a whole, there is none where one finds so many villas so closely interwoven with one another, and where the Italian villa can be studied to greater advantage.

The villas Aldobrandini and Conti are the most important.

The former has to some extent been kept up, and is now in a comparative state of completeness, but, unfortunately, where the earlier architectural work has given out, it has been replaced by something that has been considered florid and in bad taste, the result being far from harmonious. The arrangement of the terraces at the back and front of the house is very remarkable,

A wood path, Villa Aldobrandini

and admirably adapted to the formation of the land. There are some interesting fountains, and the arrangement of the water-works in this villa is very elaborately carried out. The villa garden is quite shaded by enormous sycamores, and thus has of course lost its character as a flower-garden, though it has gained a certain picturesqueness and charm.

The most interesting feature of this villa is the manner in which the hill at the back of the house has been cut out and formed into an architectural semi-circle with fountains. The actual architecture of the moment is very bad, the niches and grottos being filled with colossal and grotesque figures; but if one can imagine something simpler in its place, preserving the same general outlines, the scheme has very much to commend it. It is particularly fine when viewed from the doorway of the house. The eye is led to follow the line of the fountains, through a deep cut in the trees which supplant the circular terrace, over the hill to two tall columns which mark the position of the reservoir.

The straight walk leading from the public road to the villa is charming in its perspective, but the ascent is too abrupt ever to make it of practical use, and it is good now only as an addition to the composition of the villa.

:VILLA CONTI:

THE GREAT FEATURE of this villa is the elaborate system of staircases leading from the entrance-road to the grove. These stairways line the terrace literally from one end to the other, each one approaching at a slightly different angle. The intervening spaces are packed with shrubs and flowers. The reason for making the approach to the "bosquet" so important is not quite explained. Though the effect is extremely fine of these broad stairways, their perfection of detail is not quite in harmony with the house itself, which is extremely simple, with no architectural pretensions whatever; and judging from the elaborate details of the rest of the villa, it has either replaced something more important that was destroyed, or it was put there as something temporary, and never replaced.

At the back of the grove which stretches at the back of the house is a formal and elaborate terrace with fountains, fed from the top by a series of formal waterfalls. This arrangement, though too artificial in itself, is extremely interesting and effective when seen with the morning light coming through the trees, touching the sparkling water as it comes over the falls. There is a pathway at either side of this singular series of waterfalls, and the reservoir is reached by ascending it. This reservoir is circular in form, surrounded by a beautiful balustrade, and seems to be in the midst of a wood, so dense is the plantation all about. One of the chief peculiarities of the villas at Frascati is the importance given to such reservoirs. Frequently the water has to be brought from a long distance, and before it is distributed through the fountains and watercourses it is concentrated in a large reservoir at the highest point of the villa, and of this a feature of unusual interest is made.

Steps to the terrace, Villa Conti

VILLA FALCONIERI

THE MOST ELABORATE and interesting one is at the Villa Falconieri, where the basin is formed on the side of a hill, one half being cut in, and the other side being supported by mason-work in the form of an architectural wall, the pilasters capped by large balls. There is a wide walk surrounding the reservoir, and the whole is enclosed by a line of cypresses, now grown very large, their great depth of color contrasting beautifully with the white walls and the mason-work. Another interesting feature of the Villa Falconieri is the elaborate system of walls which surrounds it. These are now very much in ruin, and in many cases quite concealed by the large growth of trees and shrubs. What remains of permanent interest are the sculptured gates of great variety of forms. Tall columns of different-colored marbles are surmounted either by the family escutcheons or by lions or some other emblems.

The chief entrance to the villa is under a great arch, and through a straight avenue of ilex-trees, direct to the arched portico of the house. The rest of the villa is, unfortunately, quite in ruins, which is the more to be regretted, as the fine site evidently once contained one of the most beautiful of the gardens of Frascati. The view of the campagna from the house is one of the most perfect. Surrounded as the villa is by walls, almost fortified, one might say, it is quite concealed from the outside, except from a great distance. This makes the surprise much greater, on entering, to find such a magnificent view of the surrounding country.

A Frascati reservoir

:VILLA MUTI:

THE VILLA MUTI had once the most varied system of flower-gardens of any villa in Italy. The house is literally surrounded by them, all at different levels, and one might walk out of any story of the house and find one's self in a charming garden. The villa has now gone to almost absolute decay, and only the vaguest outlines of the arrangements of these gardens can be discovered. There is therefore very little there which could be so reproduced as to convey any idea of what they had been. The "bosquet" is on a terrace resting above the upper garden, and is reached by a fine stairway, which begins in full sunlight and ends in the heart of the grove in the densest shade. The reservoir is above this, and has seats about it. A great deal of terracing was necessary for gardens. The old gates and stairways which connected the terraces and the retaining wall which supported them are still in their places, and it is by this means that one reconstructs the villa, and forms a vision of the beauty of the place.

There are two villas in Frascati belonging to the Borghese family, one of which, the Villa Taverna, has been kept up as a family residence, and the other, Mondragone, is now occupied by a Jesuit school. The palace and the scale of the gardens of the latter are of great size; but with the exception of a fine terrace in front of the house, and an avenue of cypresses which leads up to it from the public road, there is nothing left but architectural details. The walls and fountain of the old garden still exist, and also a pavilion and colonnade of remarkable dignity at one end of it; but the razed parterre is now used as a playground for boys.

The Villa Taverna has a very charming flower-garden, which is reached from one wing of the house. It is raised above the road, and is, in fact, so enclosed and supported by architecture that it seems to be literally an apartment of the house. The central fountain here is a very handsome one, surrounded by laurels cut in a circular form. There are some interesting fountains let into the wall, and the balustrade which connects the garden and the house is a very good one. Beyond this there is little here to detain one, though a path which leads from the house to the grove is interesting on account of the unusual open character given it by the use of deciduous trees—something quite unusual in Italian villas.

There are other interesting corners to be studied in the minor villas at Frascati—a small flower-garden here and an ilex walk there, and fountains and abrupt stairways and architectural details; but the great charm of the villas at Frascati in their now dilapidated condition is in their beautiful sites, placed as they are high above the campagna.

With such magnificent views, and with slopes so delightfully accidental, it seems it would be difficult for an artist-gardener not to produce beautiful results, particularly as the Italians in their construction of summer villas rarely allowed ideas of convenience to interfere with their desire to produce a beautiful effect.

VILLA·FALCONIERI

ON THE OTHER SIDE of Rome, in the opposite direction from Frascati, there were some extremely interesting villas, but the lowness of the land and the unhealthy character of the campagna have long made them uninhabitable, and in most cases all that remain of them are interesting ruins in the midst of fields and pastures. Percier and Fontaine have made restoration of some of these, and it was in the author's vain endeavors to discover the site of the Villa Sachetti that one much less important in itself was discovered, but so compact, admirable, and simple in its adjustment to a small area of land that it was thought worthy of a particularly careful study. This is another Villa Falconieri, though in no way connected with the one at Frascati. It is not distinguished by an elaborateness of architecture or by the extent of its gardening, but is rather something of a compromise between the villa of a nobleman and the residence of a wealthy farmer. Its peculiarities are due to the fact that the gardens and plantations in relation to the house do not cover a width of more than four hundred feet, being in the

The entrance, Villa Falconieri

centre of a large farm, and allowing the land for farm cultivation to come almost within a stone's-throw of the house itself without being visible, or to any extent intefering with the effect of the gardens. The whole plan is in a direct straight line, so that upon entering the gate at the road one can look along the path and under the arched doorway of the house directly to the architectural feature which terminates the villa grounds. The flower-garden is on the side of the house away from the road, and at either side of a path which leads from the house to a circular terrace; this terrace contains fountains, and overlooks the valley which intervenes between it and smaller terraces on the other side. At the lowest point in this small valley is a fountain, and steps rise from this point in both directions, these steps being flanked by high hedges. At right angles with the first circular terrace are two ilex walks which form a screen for the uninteresting fields and tilled land which otherwise would be visible from the house, and this is also repeated on the street side, save that here the ilex-trees are planted radiating from the front door and leading to other lines of trees which mark the boundary. The whole plan of the villa is well held together by a system of stone-pines, which are planted at intervals, ending in a group of circular form at the extreme end. The builders of this villa were evidently fortunate in their excavations, for they have an extremely interesting collection of old Roman statuary and carved stone, which they have made the basis of the very simple architectural features of their plan. The house itself is very simple in character, with two pigeon-towers on either side, and one feels about this place as if it were intended to be lived in all the year round by its owner, and not simply a place to fly to occasionally from the busier life of the town.

Still farther on in the same direction are the ruins of the Villa Madama, but so complete here is the general wreck that nothing is to be found which in its actual state could more than suggest its former grandeur. The house itself was one of unusual architectural beauty, and there is perhaps enough left now in the gardens and terraces to show how admirably and harmoniously the villa was planned. But further study here would be altogether a matter of research, and therefore beyond the province of this book.

View of the villa and garden, Villa Falconieri

Ascent to the reservoir, Villa Falconieri

VILLA PORTICI

IN SOUTHERN ITALY very little is to be found of interest to the student of the Renaissance garden. There are, indeed, bits here and there of interest in themselves, but nothing sufficiently complete to bear the character of a design. This is the case in the royal villa at Portici, now turned into an agricultural school. The architectural details bear the mark of the eighteenth century, though it is very probable that the plan, which is excellent, would date from a much earlier time. The flower-garden behind the palace is now filled with botanical specimens, arranged without regard to the design of the parterre, but the wall is extremely interesting on account of its simplicity and the form it gives to the general outlines of the garden. The gate through which one passes from here to the grove is very picturesque, the dignified columns and delicate iron-work contrasting with the deep green of the ilexes. Looking from the garden through this gate, the grove itself presents an effect of the densest shade imaginable, partly owing to the fact that from neglect the paths in the wood have been allowed to cover them-

The bosquet, Villa Portici

selves with moss, so that everything there is green. When one has passed through the gate and is in the grove, the great variety of green is exceedingly delightful; the only relief from it which one needs is found in the high gray wall forming a part of the tennis-court, which is reached by an arched door-way in the centre of the wall. Here is nothing but ruin; but by a little study the outlines of a capital arrangement for such a place may be traced. The north side of the court is made up of a series of stone steps somewhat similar to those in the Piazza di Siena in the Villa Borghese, made for the accommodation of spectators of minor importance who viewed the games. At either end of the court are pavilions to accommodate the royal guests and and others of importance. One of them is higher than the other, and is reached by a flight of steps. At present these buildings are without roofs, and in a great state of dilapidation, their only occupants being the birds of the neighborhood.

Garden gate, Villa Portici

CAPRAROLA

THE RUINS of the gardens of Caprarola are in the same part of the country as the Villa Lante, not far from Viterbo. They contain less now for the student of gardening than for the architect, though the general plan is still visible. The relation of one thing to another is so good that the enthusiast will find a careful study of the complete design very instructive. The casino overlooks the flower-garden, its first floor being on the same level as the parterre, the second story on a level with the upper terrace, which was once enlivened with fountains, and from which there is a magnificent view of the surrounding country. In its present state of ruin, while there is much that one may see with interest, there is very little in a state to be reproduced, the most striking feature being lines of hermæ, nymphs, and satyrs which form part of the wall surrounding the flower-garden. Although these grotesque figures are characteristic of a certain tendency of Italian garden architecture, to look well they should be very much enveloped in foliage, and this, it is to be hoped, is the treatment they received when these gardens were kept up. At

79

Garden wall, Villa Caprarola

present they are singularly out of harmony with the architectural details of the casino, and one has to see them as a part of the whole scheme, and particularly from above, to be able to judge of their effect in a complete garden.

BOBOLI GARDENS

THE BEST GARDENS existing to-day in Florence and its neighborhood are due to the influence of the Medici family. Among these, the Boboli, constructed in relation to the Pitti Palace, are the largest and most important, although they cannot be said to be the most beautiful. To one thoroughly imbued with the charm of the compact treatment of the best villas about Rome, the large scale and the endless paths and avenues of Boboli are at first a shock, recalling the enormous stretches of great parks in France, although they do not in reality cover a very large area. Here interminable avenues in relentless straight lines climb one hill after another, and the visitor wanders about the place with an increasing sense of fatigue. If, however, he does not allow this fatigue to get the better of him, he will discover much that is charming in the details of the arrangements, and much that will remove his first sense of disappointment. The amphitheatre at the back of the palace is admirably adapted to the form of the hill-side, and the circular terraces which surround the most elevated of the ponds seem a natural formation, so exactly do they fit in with their surroundings. The Boboli Gardens, however, are so well known, and have been so thoroughly photographed, it seems unnecessary to treat them in detail here, particularly as there are other villas near at hand which one would find more interesting and characteristic of the Italian garden.

Gateway, Boboli Gardens

CASTELLO

THE VILLA CASTELLO is about three miles from Florence, and built in a gently undulating country. The flower-garden is its interesting feature, and it is one of the most beautiful in Italy. It covers a large area—several acres—and is placed at the back and north of the palace, on rising ground. It is protected at the north by an architectural terrace, above which is a grove of ilex and cypress trees. A large fountain marks the centre of the parterre, with circular seats and statuary surrounding it. In the centre of the terrace, at the north, is a grotto and fountain very remarkable and dignified in character. An orangery forms a part of the east wall. The arrangement of the flower-beds is as simple as possible, and the effect of the whole is very full in regard to the plantation, and very remarkable as to bloom, for so large a garden. One is conscious only of the principal paths, so well concealed is the necessary net-work of small ones by which the gardener reaches his plants. The arrangement of vines on the high stucco wall is an exceedingly good one—the lower part of it covered with climbing-roses, which are fastened to it with slender bamboo sticks attached to the wall, and the upper part for grape-vines, which, having grown up to a point above the roses, are made to grow laterally in lines one above the other, forming a sort of frieze. The grove of Castello is reached by two stairways, one at either end of the terrace. It is quite unpretentious in character, its one embellishment being a fountain, now very much overgrown with moss.

Quite near Castello is the Villa Petræa, another seat of the Medici. Here the flower-garden is in front of the house, being semicircular, with a high hedge at the north, and a terrace forming its southern limit. The abrupt nature of the hill-side is, however, ill adapted to form a flower-garden, and it has long since been filled with trees and shrubs, so that at present it is more interesting from the point of view of horticulture than that of design.

There are many interesting small gardens surrounding Florence, most of them being occupied by their owners, and are somewhat difficult of access to a stranger. If, however, he is fortunate enough to gain admittance, he will find something of interest in almost every one. This is the case also in the neighborhood of Siena; and while no one of these gardens is of great importance, they have a character as a whole which one should study to get a complete idea of Italian gardening. The gardens of Genoa are particularly worthy of study from this point of view. The character of the landscape here is extremely abrupt, and great ingenuity has been shown by the architects in planning villas in harmony with their surroundings. In the city itself each of the palaces has its own small garden, sometimes on the terrace reached from the wing, but more frequently above the main part of the palace, and reached by intricate and varied stairways. Formerly the gardens of the more important of these palaces stretched to the shore of the harbor; but with Genoa's prosperity these have now almost completely disappeared, to

Terrace wall, Villa Castello

make place for new quays and streets and other improvements of a modern city. Of the two or three remaining ones the Rosazza has the most marked characteristics of a Genoa garden. Made on the extremely abrupt slope at the north side of the harbor, the paths and terraces and fountains rise one above another, and are very skilfully planned, and so interwoven with the sharp angle of the hill-side that one is surprised to feel it the most natural place in the world for gardening. The architecture in the terraces and fountains is of a late and florid period, but so great is the mass of flowers that it is sufficiently concealed to become interesting.

GIUSTI GARDEN

THE IMPRESSION left by this garden is one of great tangle, and of a profusion of growing things mixed with the most charming garden statuary. On entering through the palace, one finds one's self in a broad avenue of cypresses; to the left is the flower-garden, and to the right a grove, arranged in open spaces among the trees, with fountains as centres. At the end of the cypress walk is a high and very precipitous hill-side, which forms the background of the garden, and is densely covered with evergreen trees and shrubs. On this hill-side one catches glimpses here and there of architectural construction, and at the top is a small temple, with a terrace which overlooks the garden and house, and beyond that the City of Verona. The garden has been allowed to go very much to ruin in its details. Few of the old fountains are running, many of them being filled up with earth and planted with flowers, sometimes with a statue marking its centre. It was very difficult in this garden to get a view which seemed to give a true impression of the place, or which in any way revealed the design. In looking down from

The Giusti Garden

above there were too many trees in the way to make this possible, and from below there was no point at a sufficient distance to see the parterre as a whole. The statuary of this garden is particularly charming, being mostly of nymphs in flowing garments, giving a festive character very much in harmony with the gayety which one looks for in such a place. In one's mind they make an agreeable contrast with the Roman senators and headless deities which do duty in most of the old Roman gardens.

CONCLUSION

IN CLOSING these brief notes descriptive of the gardens of Italy, the writer would like to add, with a view of tempering criticism, that they should be taken purely as supplementary to the illustrations. It has not been the purpose to make a treatise on landscape-gardening, but a simple attempt to show some of the most salient of the existing features of the formal garden as they may be seen to-day in Italy. Doubtless some of the villas are worthy of greater study than has been given them, and some which have been left out altogether might have claim to a place here; but it is thought that those considered are sufficient to give a comprehensive idea of the methods of the Italian in the treatment of the garden. With the general interest that undoubtedly exists in the subject of gardening to-day, it is hoped that this work may be of value towards a more thorough understanding and appreciation of the reasons which led to a formal treatment of the garden; and as there is a great similarity in the character of the landscape in many parts of our country with that of Italy, that it might lead to a revival of the same method.

PART II

Al fresco: An Overview of Charles A. Platt's

ITALIAN GARDENS

by
Keith N. Morgan

SEVERAL COLLEAGUES have assisted in the development of this text. I wish to thank Naomi Miller and Mirka Benes for their insightful criticism of the manuscript, and Kim Sichel and Dan Younger for their advice on landscape photography and the photographic book.

ITALIAN GARDENS (1894) was the first illustrated publication in English on this topic and the launching pad for Charles A. Platt (1861–1933) as the premier American practitioner of the formal garden revival. Platt achieved national significance consecutively as an etcher, painter, landscape designer, and architect, ultimately finding country house design to be the perfect combination of his multiple talents.[1] When he wrote *Italian Gardens*, he still thought of himself as a landscape painter with a secondary interest in landscape architecture and its history. His route to a career in the young profession of landscape architecture, through earlier careers in etching and painting, is reflected in the visual information and descriptions that Platt produced for *Italian Gardens*. The purpose of this republication of Platt's book is to examine the background, context, and influence of this seminal publication and to make his limited-edition original work available again to a larger audience.

PREPARATION FOR THE TRIP

Charles Platt (Figure 1) traveled to Italy in the spring of 1892 with his youngest brother, William Platt, who was then training to become a landscape architect in the office of Frederick Law Olmsted, the country's foremost landscape designer. By inviting his brother to join in this adventure, Charles intended to exert a strong, corrective influence on William's landscape education. Charles later recalled his view of Olmsted's tutelage of his brother:

> They were not teaching him on the side of landscape architecture which interested me most—that is, the purely architectural side of it. So I decided to take him abroad and go through the great gardens of Europe with a camera, etc., prepared to study them and make drawings.[2]

FIGURE 1. Charles A. Platt, self-portrait.

Though Charles may have used William's education as one excuse for this trip, he had seen some of the villas during a tour of Italy in 1886 and had already begun to design houses and gardens that clearly evoked this image.

On 30 January 1892, Olmsted wrote to his friend Charles Eliot Norton, professor of fine arts at Harvard College, asking him to advise William Platt in advance of embarking for Italy. Norton had been a critical advocate of Italian culture for nearly four decades and was the obvious counselor for the Platt tour. Olmsted explained that the two Platts were bound for Europe

> with the intention of obtaining material by sketching and photography for a volume of which an appropriate title might be *Al fresco*: its contents being designed to be mainly if not exclusively illustrations of gardens and garden furniture, seats, fountains, terraces, staircases, pergolas, rustic paths and other amorettes of Italian out of door life.[3]

While Olmsted was reluctant to permit an interruption of William's training, he agreed that his apprentice would benefit from the "necessarily close and contemplative observation of so many objects and compositions of a picturesque character, . . . and because of a certain valuable practice and this in the line of his intended calling that he is likely to obtain by sketching."[4]

Though it is impossible to know exactly what Norton told Platt or even whether they actually met, Olmsted's opinions are easily understood in the tone of his letter to Norton and in the note that he wrote to William two days later in New York:

> I am afraid that I do not think much of the fine and costly gardening of Italy, and yet I am enthusiastic in my enjoyment of much roadside foreground scenery there in which nature contends with and is gaining upon the art of man. I urge you again to hunt for beauty in commonplace and pleasant conditions; rustic terraces, old footpaths with stairs

and walls and gateways; rustic stables, sheds, winepresses, tileries, mills, pergolas and trellises, seats and resting places . . . .[5]

Olmsted was obviously determined to warn his pupil against the seductiveness of the Italian garden as a formal type. The repetition of the words "rustic" and "picturesque" is tremendously important in understanding the landscape prejudices of Olmsted and his generation and the major changes that the Platt brothers' trip and subsequent publications would inaugurate.

THE PICTURESQUE AND THE BEAUTIFUL

Platt and Olmsted viewed the landscape through very different lenses. Olmsted had begun his landscape career in 1857 as the superintendent and co-designer with Calvert Vaux of New York City's Central Park.[6] After the Civil War, he became the leading designer of public grounds—parks and residential subdivisions—as well as numerous private estates. Between the designs for Central Park and his retirement from active practice in 1895, Olmsted and his associates executed approximately 3,000 designs for landscaped spaces.[7] Olmsted's philosophy of landscape design was derived ultimately from the eighteenth-century English codification of the Picturesque— rough, irregular, and suddenly varied forms—which he used to create a naturalized landscape.[8] Added to this formula was the moral interpretation of visual form espoused by John Ruskin, the nineteenth-century English critic, who sought the Hand of God in natural landscape and believed that the imitation of nature was morally uplifting. Olmsted embraced this ideal and added his personal concern for the betterment of society through the introduction of naturalized open space, especially in burgeoning American cities. Olmsted used the more ruggedly natural forms of the Picturesque ideal to provide the greatest escape from the urban grid.

As a landscape painter and etcher, Charles Platt had also been originally indoctrinated into the cult of the Picturesque, but he reversed his aesthetic viewpoint during the mid 1880s while studying painting in Paris. Platt reported to his family in 1886, while on his first visit to Italy:

> I think it is often difficult to separate the beautiful from what is curious and extraordinary. . . . I find that I carry with me longer & with constantly recurring charm the impression of something beautiful, while the effect of the wonderful & curious & seemingly picturesque may be remembered just as long but never with the same pleasure.[9]

Platt's desertion of the Picturesque for the Beautiful was the first step in a process that led him and many of his generation to appreciate the architectural forms of the Italian garden and the classical vocabulary for houses and landscapes. Olmsted remained more attracted to the Picturesque and its expression in naturalized landscapes until the very end of his life.

By the time of Charles and William Platt's departure for Italy, however, even the Olmsted office was involved with two important commissions that indicated changes in the nature of landscape design for that firm and for America in general. The World's Columbian Exposition, held in Chicago in 1893, and Biltmore (Figure 2), the enormous estate then underway for George Washington Vanderbilt at Asheville, North Carolina, were Olmsted's personal concerns at this point. Both required a more architectonic approach to landscape design than Olmsted had previously favored. Ironically, Olmsted also sailed for Europe later in the spring of 1892, feeling the need to see some European gardens as background for his plans for the Chicago Fair.

FIGURE 2. Frederick Law Olmsted (Olmsted, Olmsted & Eliot), Biltmore, George Washington Vanderbilt estate, Asheville, North Carolina, 1890–95. Courtesy of the National Park Service, Frederick Law Olmsted National Historic Site.

THE TRIP

The exact dates of the Platt brothers' tour of Italy are not recorded, but they left soon after 1 February 1892 and returned before the middle of July of that year. For Charles, this tour was his second extended visit to Italy, for he had spent several months in the spring and summer of 1886 traversing the peninsula. A list of twenty-four gardens visited by the Platts can be determined from the labeled photographs mounted in albums after their return and from the surviving photographic negatives. Logically, they concentrated on the villas and gardens in and surrounding Rome, including Frascati, Tivoli, Bagnaia, and

Caprarola, but they also traveled to Florence, Siena, and Verona, to judge from the sites discussed in the book. Although they planned to measure, draw, and photograph these gardens, none of the measured drawings from this trip have been found.[10] Correspondence reporting the success and progress of this venture has also disappeared. Charles stopped in Paris on their return trip; William returned alone and, while vacationing in Portland, Maine, was drowned in a sailing accident on 16 July 1892.[11]

Despite the tragic death of William, to whom he was deeply attached, Charles proceeded to publish the results of their travels and observations. *Harper's Magazine*, which had been interested in Platt's work as an etcher since the early 1880s, readily accepted a two-part article concerning formal gardening in Italy, "Italian Gardens," which appeared in the July and August issues of 1893.[12] In advance of the article's publication, Harper & Brothers signed a contract with Platt on 17 April 1893 for a book. He was to supply, "free of charge, a water color drawing to be reproduced as a frontispiece . . . and matter to the amount of one thousand words in addition to that which is to appear in *Harper's Magazine*."[13] Harper & Brothers also promised to reproduce between fifteen and twenty full-page illustrations, as well as those to be used in the magazine. The book, *Italian Gardens*, appeared the following year.

THE BOOK

Italian Gardens consists of photographs, etchings, and drawings accompanied by nineteen brief, impressionistic essays on Italian gardens. Platt freely admitted that the illustrations were more important than the text. Except for three historic print views, he produced the visual documentation for the book and the earlier article. These consist of a watercolor frontispiece, several pencil drawings and one etching, cartouche chapter titles, and most importantly, photographs, some of which he retouched, making them resemble his watercolor drawings. Nearly 100 of Platt's large-format glass negatives from this trip have survived and many have been reprinted for this edition, including a selection of twenty photographs which Platt never published but which he maintained in his collection of negatives and in the photograph albums for his architectural office. These previously unseen images help to explain the range of Platt's visual experience in Italy and suggest how this trip and its record continued to influence his work and that of his generation.

THE PHOTOGRAPHS

Platt understood that his photographic record was one of the unique advantages of this book. The only publication on Italian gardens that Platt refers to in his text is Percier and Fontaine's 1809 book on the villas of Rome, *Choix des plus célèbres maisons de plaisance de Rome et de ses environs* (Figure 3), but as Platt goes on to admit in his introduction: "The art of photography has been perfected since their treatment of the subject, and the object of the present writer has been by its means to illustrate, as far as possible, the existing state of the more important gardens in Italy." Architectural and topographical photographs of Italian sites had been commercially available from the 1850s onward through such successful houses as the Alinari Brothers in Florence or Giorgio Sommers in Naples. Platt himself purchased photographs, such as the ones from Edizioni Brogi that appear in his office photograph albums, and alludes to sites that have been frequently photographed, such as the Boboli Gardens in Florence, but he fully recognized the importance of

FIGURE 3. Villa Lante, Bagnaia, from Charles Percier and Auguste Fontaine, *Choix des plus célèbres maisons de plaisance de Rome et de ses environs* (Paris: 1809). Courtesy of the Rotch Library, Massachusetts Institute of Technology.

the visual record he had assembled and published on the designed landscape of Italy.

His photographs of Italian gardens are the only serious effort by Platt to invade the evolving world of art photography. Though he was a novice in the use of photographic equipment, he brought to bear here the prejudices of landscape composition that he had perfected as a painter and etcher. He placed his camera to capture axial or diagonal entries into these gardens and frequently emphasized details or vignettes. Photographic books on landscape topics—such as the studies of Yosemite and other parks by Eadweard Muybridge and Carleton Watkins or the visual records of colonial New England's surviving domestic landscape—were certainly a familiar component of the American publishing industry from the 1860s onward. Platt's particular topic and his art-for-art's-sake philosophy, however, place *Italian Gardens* apart from the mainstream of American photographic books of the 1890s. One is tempted, rather, to relate Platt's landscape negatives to the haunting images of the French chateaux produced by Eugene Atget from the turn of the century onward. Like Atget (Figure 4), Platt had documentary intentions and similarly focused on both the long-range vista or the small detail or element. Unlike Atget, however, Platt amassed a modest archive of Italian garden images and frequently retouched the photographic plates, at least among those he published. Although he certainly was not aware of the importance these photographs would have for his subsequent work as an architect and landscape designer, he did provide the genesis of a professional photographic archive here. Platt's architectural design process began from consultation of these mounted photographs, whose margins provided the first place to record ideas for design challenges as small as a molding profile or as large as a garden pavilion or a principal elevation (Figure 5).

FIGURE 4. Eugene Atget, Versailles, Cyparisse par Flamen, 1902. Albumen-silver print, 9⅜ × 7″. Collection, The Museum of Modern Art, New York. Abbott-Levy Collection. Partial gift of Shirley C. Burden.

107

FIGURE 5. Doorway, Villa Falconieri, Frascati, from the Italian Garden Photograph Album, Charles A. Platt Library, Century Association, New York.

"Leaving out the matter of research altogether," as Platt candidly admits, his ahistorical perspective informed the presentation of opinions and information, as well as the choice of visual images. Indeed, Platt probably never entered a library in preparing for the trip or for the subsequent publication. He believed that his mission was to reveal the existing state of Italian villas for the lessons they could teach, rather than to reconstruct as an archaeologist the original configuration of the villas.

Platt began with the Villa Lante at Bagnaia, not because it was the finest or the earliest of Italian villas but because, in Platt's opinion, it was the best-preserved example and could most quickly explain the nature of the villa type. He next turned to the villas of Rome and the surrounding countryside, discussing sixteenth- through eighteenth-century examples. He was generally attracted to the earlier sites and was highly critical of the "bad" and "grotesque" architecture of the Baroque villas of Frascati. Platt gives only passing attention to the villas of Tuscany, which later writers, such as Edith Wharton, would emphasize as the starting point for the Renaissance villa. He dismisses southern Italy, where "very little is to be found of interest to the student of the Renaissance garden," and he avoids most of the North, including the flamboyant villas of the Italian Lakes.

Throughout, he emphasizes the conception of the villa as a comprehensive unit that embraces the house, the flower garden, the terrace, the grove, the fountain, and the water system, all intimately interrelated. He frequently uses details or vignettes, what Olmsted had referred to as "amorettes," to explain the macrocosm: "There are many architectural details of interest in the Villa Borghese, some fine gates and fountains and stone benches." He neglects to illustrate plans of the villas, with the exception of two historical prints. Nevertheless, he frequently discusses the spatial configuration of the site and celebrates the creation of integrated outdoor living spaces as a glory of the Italian garden. At the Quirinal Gardens he notes that "the great height of the hedges which once marked the borders of the beds have now turned these enclosures into most charming apartments." And further, "to one who doubts the advantage of straight lines in gardening, the extreme beauty of the perspective in the Quirinal would teach much." He complains about the changes that have been made in the form and planting of the Villa Mattei under the influence of later fashion in horticulture: "The result has been to give its general appearance one without character as a complete work of art, the contrast between the formal and the so-called neutral methods filling one with a sense of lost opportunity." His enthusiasm for the formal arrangement of the gardens over the "so-called neutral" or natural style of planting is constantly reinforced.

A revealing and surprising focus throughout his notes and illustration is the prominence given to the flower gardens of the villas. At the Villa Borghese, he even finds the absence of one worthy of note: "There is no large flower-garden making a feature in itself, though at the time the villa was kept up a great many flowers were grown throughout the place." In Rome he declares, "for a flower-garden, pure and simple, there is none more charming in Italy than the Colonna," and he extols the charm of the cutting garden at the Villa Mattei for its straightforward organizational scheme, where everything is designed for convenience. The circular basin in its center is used to water the plants, and the wide path in the middle of the garden affords easy access to the raised beds. Geometry must be softened by plantings, however; at the Villa Albani, Platt complains that the strict manicure of the parterre has been made "altogether unpleasant by its hardness" and cautions that "to look well under these conditions very full planting is absolutely necessary." When Platt turned his hand to landscape design, he emphasized gardens where abundant flowers spilled over the rectilinear shapes of paths and architecture.

Platt's favorite villa from this trip was the smallest and least well known of those he discussed. In the low-lying and then unhealthy district north of Rome, Platt happened upon a site that would hold his imagination for many years:

> It was in the author's vain endeavors to discover the site of the Villa Sachetti that one much less important in itself was discovered, but so compact, admirable, and simple in its adjustment to a small area of land that it was thought worthy of a particularly careful study.

Platt was fascinated by this property, which he saw as a compromise between "the villa of a nobleman and the residence of a wealthy farmer," a site so narrow that it was no wider than 400 feet at any point, with the fields and vineyards immediately adjacent. A drawing of the plan of this villa (Figure 6), variously called the Villa Costanzi, Sardegna, or Falconieri (as he refers to it in *Italian Gardens*), may have been a reworking of the measured drawings made during the 1892 trip. Platt was attracted to this villa because its scale, compactness, and directness of design were of great value for study and emulation by Americans.

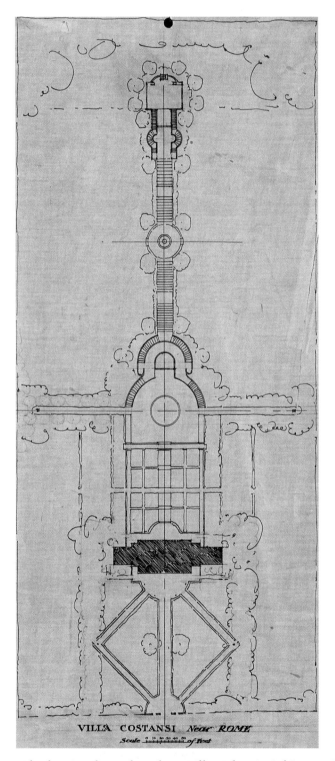

VILLA COSTANSI *Near ROME*
Scale of Feet

FIGURE 6. Charles A. Platt, plot plan, Villa Falconieri (Costanzi), near Rome, 1912. Photograph by Richard Cheek.

Platt's article and book also fit into a pattern of increasing American interest in Italy throughout the second half of the nineteenth century. Nathaniel Hawthorne and other writers popularized Italy at mid century; Charles Eliot Norton's *Notes of Travel and Study in Italy* (1860) added an informed criticism of Italian art and culture. Henry James claimed Italy for his own from the novel *Roderick Hudson* (1875) onward.[14] But for the English-speaking community, as Platt claims in the introduction to *Italian Gardens*, "there is no existing work of any great latitude treating the subject of gardens." The publication of Platt's book anticipated by almost a decade an avalanche of American writing on Italian landscape design. In 1902, Janet Ross' *Florentine Villas* and A. Holland Forbes' *Architectural Gardens of Italy* marked the emergence of a widespread interest in Italian gardens that would continue through the 1920s, gradually becoming more scholarly and less effusive.[15]

The best-known early work in this series was Edith Wharton's *Italian Villas and Their Gardens* (1904), significant for Wharton's research and descriptive facility as well as the charming illustrations by Maxfield Parrish (Figure 7). Interestingly, Wharton did not include *Italian Gardens* among the titles in her brief bibliography though she would definitely have known of it through Maxfield Parrish, Platt's friend and summer neighbor, whose father, Stephen Parrish, had originally taught Platt the technique of etching. One clue to Platt's omission may be found in Wharton's opening statement: "Italian garden-craft . . . is independent of floriculture." This, of course, is in direct opposition to Platt's interest in and description of flowers and color in Italian gardens. Indeed, even Wharton's title would have been unacceptable to Platt, who believed that the term "villa" automatically incorporated

V I L L A   P I A

FIGURE 7. Maxfield Parrish, Villa Pia—In the Gardens of the Vatican, from Edith Wharton, *Italian Villas and Their Gardens* (New York: 1904).

the garden as well as the house.

Unlike Platt, however, Wharton functioned as an historian. She organized her material in a manner to suggest the chronological and geographical evolution of the Italian villa. Platt had relied solely upon the visual research of Percier and Fontaine's elegant reconstructions of Roman villas; Wharton, on the other hand, consulted and cited scholarship in English, French, German, and Italian. Although Wharton allowed there were "not a few resemblances between the North American summer climate and that of Italy in spring and autumn," she was critical of recent attempts to emulate Italian garden principles in America.[16] Platt, by contrast, concluded his text with this hope: "As there is a great similarity in the character of the landscape in many parts of our country with that of Italy, . . . it might lead to a revival of the same method." By the time Wharton's book was published, Platt's writings and garden commissions had introduced in America a formal garden revival inspired by the Italian villa.

CRITICAL REACTION

Italian Gardens may have launched Platt's career as a landscape architect, but it was not greeted with universal acceptance. *Garden and Forest*, the principal organ of the landscape and horticultural professions in America at that time, had alerted its readers as early as 2 November 1892 to the forthcoming article on "the Old gardens of Italy by Mr. Charles A. Platt, the well-known landscape painter and etcher."[17] The magazine's ultimate reaction to the essays, however, was one of mild disappointment. Allowing that "much of the interest which invests these pictures . . . is derived from the fact that [the gardens] are, in a measure, ruined,"[18] the reviewer goes on to state that only in the American South would such gardens be climatically appropriate. He continues:

> But after all, works of this kind only appeal to the aesthetic sense; they delight the eye and satisfy the cultivated taste as a beautiful piece of tapestry or pottery does. It is beauty for its own sake. It expresses no sentiment and carries no inner meaning; it does not address itself to the nobler part of our nature as simple natural scenery does.[19]

Following the moral philosophy espoused by John Ruskin, Charles Eliot Norton, and Frederick Law Olmsted, *Garden and Forest* was more concerned with the legitimacy of the Italian garden as a landscape type for America than with Platt's treatment of the subject. "Beauty for its own sake" without "inner meaning" was still suspect.

When the material appeared in book form, Charles Eliot, then a partner in the office of Olmsted, Olmsted & Eliot and the creator of the Boston Metropolitan Park Commission, mounted a harsher and more exacting attack on Platt's book:

> The text of the book is very handsomely printed with wide margins, but consists of the briefest notes. Even if it is "taken purely as supplementary to the illustrations," as we are asked to take it, it is unsatisfactory. For the fairly-to-be-expected elucidation of the plates, plans (as well as fuller notes) are sadly needed, yet only one is provided. On the first page, mention is made of the great book of Percier and Fontaine, and it is stated that there exists no other "work of any great latitude" treating Italian gardens. Evidently our author is not acquainted with W. P. Tuckermann's "Die Gartenkunst der Italienischen Renaissance-Zeit," published in 1884, and containing besides the twenty plates and numerous other cuts, some twenty ground-plans and cross-sections of Renaissance villas.[20]

Though Eliot's criticisms were fully justified, Platt's purpose, as he repeatedly stated, was not to provide an historical assessment. Percier and Fontaine, whose monumental tome Platt had presumably consulted, produced elaborate plates (Figure 3) that influenced the image of Renaissance Rome throughout most of the nineteenth century. Tuckermann, of whose work Platt was probably ignorant, published a variety of illustrations, including the detailed plans borrowed from Percier and Fontaine (Figure 8) that Eliot admired and felt Platt should have included. The art-for-art's-sake mentality that *Garden and Forest* criticized in the Platt book was exactly the basis on which Platt made his visual evaluation of design characteristics as they survived in the gardens he visited. Indeed, the soft-focus character of Platt's photographs may be seen as an excellent match for the soft-focus methodology of his analysis, and the book fits perfectly within the artistic philosophy of Platt's rising generation.

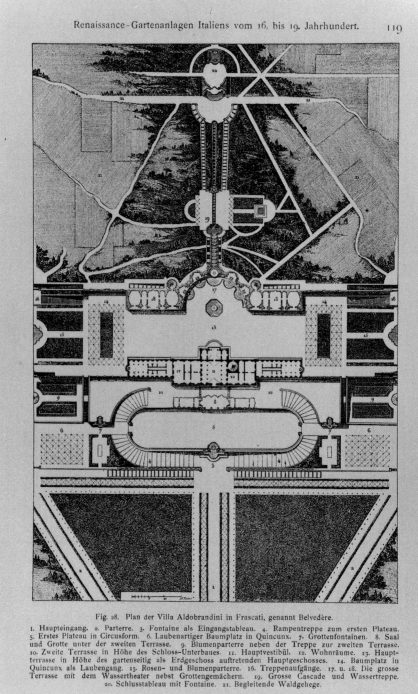

Fig. 28. Plan der Villa Aldobrandini in Frascati, genannt Belvedère.

1. Haupteingang. 2. Parterre. 3. Fontaine als Eingangstableau. 4. Rampentreppe zum ersten Plateau. 5. Erstes Plateau in Circusform. 6. Laubenartiger Baumplatz in Quincunx. 7. Grottenfontainen. 8. Saal und Grotte unter der zweiten Terrasse. 9. Blumenparterre neben der Treppe zur zweiten Terrasse. 10. Zweite Terrasse in Höhe des Schloss-Unterbaues. 11. Hauptvestibül. 12. Wohnräume. 13. Hauptterrasse in Höhe des gartenseitig als Erdgeschoss auftretenden Hauptgeschosses. 14. Baumplatz in Quincunx als Laubengang. 15. Rosen- und Blumenparterre. 16. Treppenaufgänge. 17. u. 18. Die grosse Terrasse mit dem Wassertheater nebst Grottengemächern. 19. Grosse Cascade und Wassertreppe. 20. Schlusstableau mit Fontaine. 21. Begleitende Waldgehege.

FIGURE 8. Plot plan, Villa Aldobrandini, Frascati, from W. P. Tuckermann, *Die Gartenkunst der Italienischen Renaissance-Zeit* (Berlin: 1884). Courtesy of the Massachusetts Horticultural Society Library.

THE FORMAL GARDEN REVIVAL

Platt's *Italian Gardens* was greeted with skepticism and criticism by *Garden and Forest* and elsewhere, in part, because it represented the beginning of an American parallel to the professional schism that then existed in England. There the landscape designers had taken sides in support of the dichotomous theories of William Robinson and Reginald Blomfield.[21] Robinson, primarily a plantsman, espoused reliance on naturalized garden layout and the use of hardy natives and hardy or half-hardy exotics as a formula for overcoming the artificiality of late-Victorian landscape design, especially the excesses of carpet bedding with gaudy annuals. He advanced his ideas in *The Wild Garden* (1870) and in his more influential *English Flower Garden and Home Grounds* (1883). His chief opponent was the architect Reginald Blomfield who in *The Formal Garden in England* (1892) described landscape gardening, as practiced by Robinson and his type, as the fuzzy work of amateurs. Instead, he proposed a landscape architecture of formally organized compositions (Figure 9) which he considered a true art form. Although Americans never reached the extremes of their English contemporaries, garden designers here were emphatically divided between the formal and the natural schools in the 1890s. In 1904 Edith Wharton claimed that "the cult of the Italian garden has spread from England to America," but Platt was already sketching and measuring gardens in Italy when Reginald Blomfield's book appeared. *Italian Gardens* and Platt's work as a landscape architect led to the popularization of the formal garden revival here before it occurred in Britain.[22]

The American interest was more reinforced by than derived from the work in England. Certainly, an Italianate style of gardening had emerged as a popular variant in mid nineteenth-

THE OLD GARDENS AT BRICKWALL NEAR NORTHIAM : SUSSEX

FIGURE 9. F. Inigo Thomas, The Old Gardens at Brickwall, from Reginald Blomfield, *The Formal Garden in England* (London: 1892).

century Britain, with W. A. Nesfield as its most successful practitioner. But the Robinson-Blomfield dispute raised the debate to a higher key. Actually, William Robinson's own garden at Gravetye Manor in Sussex was one that incorporated both the architectonic framework that Blomfield sought and lush plantings that Robinson popularized. A new stage in the Italian garden revival was established by Harold Peto, who had spent his boyhood at Somerleyton, Norfolk, in an Italianate garden by Nesfield and who began a personal study of the gardens of Renaissance Italy in the 1880s. Interestingly, Peto visited the United States in 1887 and his garden designs from the mid 1890s onward show the obvious influence of Platt's early designs in an Italian mode.[23]

FIGURE 10. Italian Garden, H. H. Hunnewell estate, Wellesley, Massachusetts, 1860s onward, from the sixth edition of A. J. Downing, *A Treatise on the Theory and Practice of Landscape Gardening* (New York: 1859). Courtesy of the Massachusetts Horticultural Society Library.

Just as in England, there were important American precedents for formal landscape treatment before the 1890s, especially in the environs of Boston. In the 1860s, H. H. Hunnewell began to lay out a series of formal gardens on his lakeside estate in Wellesley, Massachusetts. Using American plant material, he created an elaborate terrace garden of clipped topiary work, commonly called the Italian Garden (Figure 10). In 1885, Isabella Stewart Gardner started to develop the grounds of her forty-acre place in Brookline. Laid out as a sequence of gardens, Green Hill included vine-covered pergolas, box-edged flower gardens, pools, and fountains—intended to evoke the spirit of the Renaissance—as well as open lawns in the English natural manner and a Japanese garden with dwarf trees, all typical of the eclecticism of the late nineteenth century. One description of Green Hill noted that the garden contained many works of art: "There are statues and carved seats, there are great vases, and a fine old well head from Rome. One wall contains a number of Latin inscriptions, brought here from their hiding places in Italy."[24] As cultural high priestess of Boston, Isabella Stewart Gardner epitomized the then-current Italianate interest of the city in the building of her townhouse/museum, Fenway Court, a Venetian palazzo begun in 1898. Platt soon provided Boston and the rest of America with more sophisticated gardens derived from Italian inspiration.

THE INFLUENCE OF THE BOOK

The publication of *Italian Gardens* was merely the most public of a series of steps Platt took to create a new formula for garden design and architecture in the United States. Before leaving for Italy, Platt designed a house for Annie Lazarus, a neighbor in the summer art colony of Cornish, New Hampshire, which demonstrates that he had already seen and digested many of the lessons of the Italian villa. High Court (Figure 11), the Lazarus house, was built in 1890–91 on a hilltop just above Platt's own Cornish retreat. Platt needed the assistance of a friend, the architect Stanford White, for the details of the U-shaped, colonnaded villa he designed, but he needed no help in developing the plot plan for the property and garden. Indeed, the house suggests that Platt may have already visited the Villa Falconieri (Costanzi) and the villas of Frascati. The plan of High Court (Figure 12) bears a partial resemblance to the drawing of the Villa Falconieri (Costanzi): it too emphasizes a

FIGURE 11. Charles A. Platt, High Court, Annie Lazarus house, Cornish, New Hampshire, 1890–91.

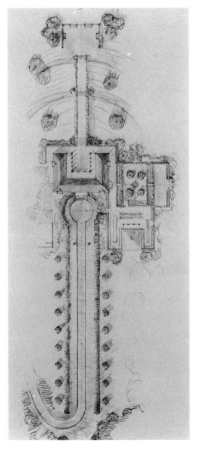

FIGURE 12. Plot plan, High Court. Photograph by Richard Cheek.

major axis through the house, introduced by a tightly controlled, narrow approach road on one side and opening out to a vista on the other. As Platt later explained, however:

> To a house set high upon a hill, the ground falling away from it with some abruptness, the whole site chosen for the view, the landscape gardener will give surroundings of the utmost simplicity that they may not compete with or disturb the larger without. This was recognized in the Frascati villas of Italy, which were terraced to give a view of the distant campagna, and in America there was an example in High Court. [25]

When Platt returned from Italy in 1892, he began the redevelopment of his own Cornish garden (Figure 13) using a series of paths to connect simple architectonic units carefully

FIGURE 13. Charles A. Platt house, Cornish, New Hampshire, 1892 onward.

defined by hedges to create separate rooms for out-of-doors living.

Over the next two decades, Platt would continue to convert the Cornish hills into the Frascati of America, inspiring other members of the artist colony, such as Augustus Saint-Gaudens and Maxfield and Stephen Parrish, to follow his example in their own gardens at Cornish. Many architects who were part of Saint-Gaudens' circle were influenced by Platt's garden-making on summer visits to Cornish. One of his earliest converts was the Detroit industrialist and Oriental art collector Charles Lang Freer (Figure 14), whom Platt met in Cornish in 1890.[26] In 1894, Platt recommended to him an itinerary for a tour of Italian gardens that Freer made in the autumn of that year, and from the late 1890s onward, Freer was one of Platt's most loyal patrons.[27]

As in England, the reemergence of the formal garden in America was logically instigated by those trained in design rather than in horticulture. In 1895, the architectural firm of Carrère & Hastings laid out Indian Harbor (Figure 15)—E. C. Benedict's estate in Greenwich, Connecticut, on the Long Island Sound—which had important parallels to Platt's work. Here Thomas Hastings structured a plot plan that Platt would have admired for its clean lines and careful integration, but the Benedict property suffered from the harsh outline that Platt had objected to at the Villa Albani. The inspiration for Indian Harbor was only partially the villas of Italy; Hastings' vision revealed more fully his training at the Ecole des Beaux-Arts and a generalized approach to the formal garden, as easily dressed in French garb as in Italian. As did Charles Follen McKim, Stanford White, and others who had been trained in Paris, Carrère & Hastings produced a rigid formula for the gardens surrounding their houses that was often archeologically tied to the stylistic image of the house it was designed to embellish.

FIGURE 14. Charles Lang Freer, Capri, 1894. Courtesy of the Freer Gallery of Art, Washington, D.C.

FIGURE 15. Thomas Hastings (Carrère & Hastings), plot plan, Indian Harbor, E. C. Benedict estate, Greenwich, Connecticut, 1895. Photograph by Richard Cheek.

A more important early commission for the popularization of the formal garden in America was the development of the grounds of Faulkner Farm, the estate of Congressman and Mrs. Charles F. Sprague in Brookline, Massachusetts.[28] Chosen after Olmsted, Olmsted & Eliot had been dismissed, Platt designed a garden and landscape setting for the existing three-story white frame house, recently designed by Little & Browne and sited near the crest of a hill. Platt's plot plan (Figure 16) included a long, straight approach drive that led into a walled forecourt on the uphill side of the house, ending in a monumental statue on axis. A terraced promenade and woodland garden (Figure 17) capped the top of the hill, with a view of the house and grounds on one side and of the Boston skyline on the other. A comparison of the plan of Faulkner Farm with that of the sixteenth-century Villa Gamberaia (Figure 19) near Settignano shows

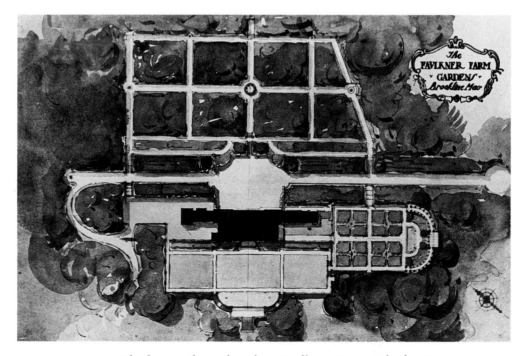

FIGURE 16. Charles A. Platt, plot plan, Faulkner Farm, Charles Sprague estate, Brookline, Massachusetts, 1897–98. Photograph by Richard Cheek.

FIGURE 17. Faulkner Farm upon its completion, 1898. Courtesy of the National Park Service, Frederick Law Olmsted National Historic Site.

FIGURE 18. Pool and arches, Faulkner Farm, 1898. Courtesy of the National Park Service, Frederick Law Olmsted National Historic Site.

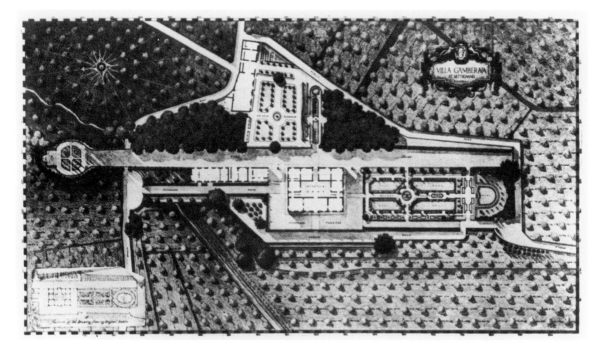

FIGURE 19. Plot plan, Villa Gamberaia, Settignano, 1610. Drawn and measured by Edward G. Lawson. Courtesy of Loeb Library, Graduate School of Design, Harvard University.

how fully Platt had absorbed the principles of Italian garden design. In *Italian Gardens*, Platt dismisses the gardens around Florence, the vicinity of Settignano, in two sentences, concluding that "while no one of these gardens is of great importance, they have a character as a whole which one should study to get a complete idea of Italian gardening."

The houses of Faulkner Farm and the Villa Gamberaia were similar in many respects. Each was sited below the crest of a hill, with nearly identical disposition of a woodland garden on the hilltop, an allée across the front of the house ending in a monumental statue, a grassed terrace behind the house, and an adjacent formal garden with a semicircular end. Platt never visited the Villa Gamberaia, yet given an identical problem and a similar site, he produced a design at Faulkner Farm that showed his mastery of the Renaissance villa concept. Faulkner Farm soon became the most frequently illustrated of Platt's early designs; it represents a pivotal moment in the emergence of the formal garden in America.

Although he had no training as an architect or landscape architect, Platt used the popularity of *Italian Gardens* and the success of his early projects in Cornish and Brookline to invade the burgeoning country house practice in America. Over the next three decades, he produced scores of elegant designs for gardens, country houses, and institutional buildings that owed their original inspiration to the lessons he had learned in Italy, especially the ideal of coordinating interior and exterior spaces, extended into the landscape. Two of the finest of his designs from the first decade of the new century demonstrate how Platt applied the Italian design sensibility to his American work. At Villasera (1903–06), the estate of the Rev. Joseph Hutcheson in Warren, Rhode Island, an Italian-derived model emerged that he would modulate on subsequent occasions. Villasera, a rectangular property situated on the Narragansett Bay, was laid out with the house placed as the pivot through which the grounds and gardens were experienced. A sight line from the entrance gates to the entrance portico focused the approach either through the house and out to the view on axis or back to the formal gardens along the left side of the house and the approach drive.

Platt handled a somewhat similar site in a very different manner for Gwinn (Figure 20), the 1908 estate of William G. Mather at Bratenahl, east of Cleveland, Ohio, on Lake Erie. Here Platt placed the house at the edge of a cliff overlooking the lake. He used the left and right edges of the property for the entrance and service drives, respectively, and placed the formal garden, greensward, and woodland garden as the buffer between the public road and the house. Such different design

FIGURE 20. Charles A. Platt, plot plan, Gwinn, William G. Mather estate, Bratenahl, Ohio, 1908. Photograph by Richard Cheek.

solutions for similar site-specific challenges nevertheless have common threads. The rules of geometry and clear spatial order are the initial impulses; both designs recall Platt's enthusiastic reaction to the Villa Falconieri (Costanzi) near Rome, which was "so compact, admirable, and simple in its adjustment to a small area of land . . . ." The many architects who were attracted to Platt's work in domestic architecture and garden design quickly realized a Platt plan invariably had unique qualities that set it apart from the commonplace.

As the scale of Platt's commissions increased and began to rival or surpass the land area of the typical villa in Italy, Platt looked more to historic models, Italian and otherwise. The most obvious example of this thrust is his design for the country estate of Harold and Edith Rockefeller McCormick at Lake Forest, north of Chicago, developed from 1908 through 1918. Called Villa Turicum, the Rockefeller McCormick place was the most conspicuously Italian of Platt's many country house designs. The influence of the Italian villa is felt most compellingly in the design for the lakefront side of the house (Figure 21), where a series of terraces are connected by a watercourse, much in the tradition of the Villa d'Este. Throughout the house and grounds there are specific quotations of villas Platt had visited in 1892. The entrance front (Figure 22) is derived from the Villa Mondragone at Frascati, which Platt did not illustrate in *Italian Gardens*, but which he photographed on this trip (Figure 23). The wall fountain in the flower garden was derived from the one at the Villa Portici. The Rockefeller McCormick estate, although it embodied the major theories behind Platt's designs, was not typical of his country houses. Its scale was immense and the money available encouraged Platt to actually reproduce rather than adapt the gardens of Italy.

FIGURE 21. Charles A. Platt, lakefront terraces, Villa Turicum, Harold and Edith Rockefeller McCormick estate, Lake Forest, Illinois, 1908–18.

FIGURE 22. Entrance elevation, Villa Turicum.

But the ascendancy of the formal garden revival had been achieved well before the construction of Villa Turicum. Within a decade after Platt's initial gardens and publications appeared, Guy Lowell, a Boston architect, documented the rise of the architectural landscape group in his 1902 book, *American Gardens*. Though he warned that changes in climate and plant material had to be judiciously considered in transposing Italian forms to the United States, Lowell concluded that "it is the appropriate adaptation of the established European principles of gardening to American surroundings that will perfect an American style."[29] The illustrations in Lowell's book show the extent to which the Italian garden formula had been embraced by American designers. According to Lowell, the leaders of the movement included key individuals in established architectural firms, such as Carrère & Hastings and McKim, Mead & White, as well as landscape architects. The most frequently illustrated works were gardens by Philadelphia architect Wilson Eyre and those by a new designer, Charles A. Platt. Even the title that Lowell chose for his book consciously demonstrates that Platt's *Italian Gardens* had launched a new American landscape tradition.

FIGURE 23 ·· Villa Mondragone, Frascati, 1892. Photograph by Charles A. Platt.

NOTES

1. The most recent treatment of Platt's life and works is my own study: Keith N. Morgan, *Charles A. Platt: The Artist as Architect* (New York: The Architectural History Foundation, Inc., and MIT Press, 1985). Passages from that text are republished here through the kind permission of the Architectural History Foundation and MIT Press. The first half of Platt's career was recorded in *A Monograph of the Works of Charles A. Platt* (New York: The Architectural Book Publishing Company, 1913).

2. Charles A. Platt to Royal Cortissoz, 30 June 1913, Platt Letter File, Cortissoz Papers, Beinecke Rare Book and Manuscript Library, Yale University. Cortissoz, an art critic, wrote the foreword for the 1913 publication on Platt's work.

3. Frederick Law Olmsted to Charles Eliot Norton, 30 January 1892, Letterpress, F. L. Olmsted Papers, Manuscript Division, Library of Congress.

4. Ibid.

5. Frederick Law Olmsted to William Platt, 1 February 1892, ibid.

6. The earliest substantial treatment of Olmsted's career is by Frederick Law Olmsted, Jr., and Theodora Kimball, *Frederick Law Olmsted: Landscape Architect 1822–1903* (New York: G. P. Putnam's Sons), in two volumes: *Early Years* (1922) and *Central Park* (1928). The past two decades have produced two major biographies of Olmsted, several museum exhibitions and catalogues, and the publication to date of four volumes of the edited papers of Frederick Law Olmsted, housed in the Manuscript Division of the Library of Congress.

7. For a list of these commissions, organized by geographic location, see *The Master List of Design Projects of the Olmsted Firm 1857–1950* (Boston: National Association for Olmsted Parks in conjunction with the Massachusetts Association for Olmsted Parks, 1987).

8. The clearest and most concise analysis of Olmsted's landscape philosophy is by Charles E. Beveridge, "Frederick Law Olmsted's Philosophy of Landscape Design," *Nineteenth Century* 3/2 (1978): 38–43.

9. Charles A. Platt to his family, 23 February 1886, Platt Family Papers, Geoffrey Platt, Bedford, N.Y.

10. "My brother and I made measurements of the essentials of the best gardens in Italy." Charles A. Platt to Royal Cortissoz, 30 June 1913, Platt Letter File, Cortissoz Papers, Beinecke Rare Book and Manuscript Library, Yale University.

11. Charles Henry Pope, *The Platt Genealogy* (Boston: C. H. Pope, 1897), 409. William Barnes Platt was born on 16 May 1868 and was twenty-four at the time of his death.

12. Before his departure to study in Paris, Platt had declined to provide a series of illustrations for articles on the hill towns of Tuscany by William Dean Howells. Joseph Pennell accepted the commission and stopped to visit Platt in Paris en route to Italy, much to the latter's annoyance. Platt believed that etching was an art form and he was concerned that the commercialization of illustrating books and periodicals exerted a negative influence on this art. It is understandable, therefore, that Platt, with one exception, did not make etchings for the *Harper's* article or subsequent book, but used photographs, drawings, and watercolors instead.

13. Contract between Harper & Brothers and Charles Platt, 17 April 1893, Charles A. Platt File, Harper & Brothers Collection, Special Collections, Columbia University Library. The contract originally called for an additional two thousand words but was altered to require only one thousand words in addition to those which would appear in *Harper's Magazine*.

14. For the most recent and comprehensive review of the fascination of American writers and artists with Rome, the focus of Platt's investigations, see William Vance, *America's Rome* (New Haven and London: Yale University Press, 1989), 2 vols.

15. For a brief discussion of the American interest in Italian gardens, see David R. Coffin's introduction to *The Italian Garden: First Dumbarton Oaks Colloquium on the History of Landscape Architecture* (Washington, D.C.: Trustees for Harvard University, 1972). In addition to the books mentioned in the text, the following are notable early works on the Italian Renaissance garden published in the United States: Julia Cartwright, *Italian Gardens of the Renaissance and Other Studies* (New York: Charles Scribner's Sons, 1914); Harold Donaldson Eberlein, *Villas of Florence and Tuscany* (Philadelphia: J. B. Lippincott, 1922); and Rose Standish Nichols, *Italian Pleasure Gardens* (New York: Dodd, Mead &

Company, 1926). Also important are American republications of English titles and translations of Italian works on Renaissance gardens. For a recent discussion of the former, see Jane Brown, "The Italian Influence" in *The English Garden in Our Times* (London: Antique Collectors Club, 1987).

16. Edith Wharton, *Italian Villas and Their Gardens* (New York: The Century Company, 1905), 6. Ironically, Wharton later built a country house called The Mount at Lenox, Massachusetts, where she, her architect Edmund Hoppin, and her niece, the landscape architect Beatrix Jones Farrand, developed the grounds and gardens in an Italian manner. For a discussion of this book's place in Wharton's career, see R. W. B. Lewis, *Edith Wharton: A Biography* (New York: Harper & Brothers, 1975), 116–121.

17. *Garden and Forest* 5 (2 November 1892): 528. This periodical was "conducted" from 1888 to 1897 by Charles Sprague Sargent, director of Harvard's Arnold Arboretum. The death of William A. Stiles, editor for much of the magazine's ten-year history, was announced in the 6 October 1897 issue, and publication ceased with the end of the calendar year. *Garden and Forest* is the best indicator of then-current ideas in the developing professions of landscape architecture, horticulture, and forestry during this important decade in America.

18. *Garden and Forest* 6 (2 August 1893): 322. A review of the first part of Platt's article, which ran in the July issue of *Harper's Magazine*, can be found in *Garden and Forest* 6 (5 July 1893): 290.

19. Ibid.

20. Charles Eliot, review of *Italian Gardens* in *The Nation* 57 (December 1893): 491. Charles Eliot was probably the best-read American on the history and current practice of landscape architecture. After a two-year apprenticeship with Frederick Law Olmsted, Eliot spent eighteen months in 1887–88 studying and traveling in Europe to complete his self-education as a landscape architect. The son of the president of Harvard College, Charles Eliot had spent considerable time in Europe as a child and read fluently several European languages. By comparison, Charles A. Platt, who did not attend college, knew French from his years in Paris as an art student, but he did not read German. It is interesting to note, however, that during his extensive travels in Europe, Eliot had not visited any of the sites that Platt dis-

cusses in his book. Like young William Platt, Eliot may have been warned off the "fine and costly gardening" of Italy by Frederick Law Olmsted. William Platt and Charles Eliot would not have been members of the Olmsted office at the same time.

21. David Ottewill, chapter 1 in *The Edwardian Garden* (New Haven and London: Yale University Press, 1989).

22. Lewis, *Edith Wharton: A Biography*, 12.

23. Ottewill, *The Edwardian Garden*, 145–156.

24. Barr Ferree, *American Estates and Gardens* (New York: Munn & Company, 1904), 289. Ferree offers a brief discussion of both the Hunnewell and Gardner gardens with multiple illustrations.

25. Aymar Embury, "Charles A. Platt: His Works," *Architecture* 26 (August 1912): 142.

26. For further information on this relationship see Keith N. Morgan, "The Patronage Matrix: Charles L. Freer, Client; Charles A. Platt, Architect," *Winterthur Portfolio* 17:2/3 (Summer/Autumn 1982): 121–134.

27. Among the early commissions that Freer brought to Platt were the 1897 design for LaSalle Gardens South, an architectonically arranged subdivision with a central, private park (the failed scheme of Frank J. Hecker, Freer's business partner) and the 1902 garden of the Yondotega Club, a private men's club in Detroit, attached to an earlier building by Albert Kahn.

28. See also Alan Emmet, "Faulkner Farm: An Italian Garden in Massachusetts," *Journal of Garden History* 6/2 (1986): 162–178.

29. Guy Lowell, introduction to *American Gardens* (Boston: Bates & Guild Co., 1902), not paginated. For a bibliography of sources on Italian-derived gardens, see Richard G. Kenworthy, "Published Records of Italianate Gardens in America," *Journal of Garden History* 10/1 (1990): 10–70.

PART III

Additional Plates by Charles A. Platt

FOREWORD TO THE PLATES

THE FOLLOWING PHOTOGRAPHS, taken by Charles A. Platt during the 1892 tour and printed from surviving negatives, are a selection of those not used in the original edition of *Italian Gardens*. The order of the illustrations has been arranged to approximate the sequence Platt used in his book, and although these villas may be more commonly known by other names today, Platt's original nomenclature for each site has been maintained. They are published for the first time here as a further indication of Platt's wide-ranging interest in the Italian villa.

These are photographs of sites and images that were influential in Platt's subsequent work as an architect and landscape architect. The sunken courtyard of the Villa Taverna at Frascati, for example, was often quoted in his later designs, and he borrowed specific details from the Villa Mondragone at Frascati for projects such as the Villa Turicum in Lake Forest, Illinois. Also included is a fresh view of the flower-garden at Rome's Colonna Gardens that Platt was so taken with, as well as a representation of the Baroque architectural extravagances he emphatically disliked in the Villa Falconieri at Frascati. The haunting images of the hedge walk at the Quirinal Gardens were later used as references by Platt for his etchings and watercolor drawings.

PLATE 1. Villa Lante, Bagnaia, pavilion from the lower garden.

PLATE 2. Villa Lante, Fountain of the Moors.

PLATE 3. Villa Lante, Fountain of the Moors.

PLATE 4. Villa Lante, three vases and steps to the second terrace.

PLATE 5. Villa Pamfili, Rome, broad stone steps.

PLATE 6. Quirinal Gardens, Rome, arched entrance to the hedge walk.

152

PLATE 7. Quirinal Gardens, hedge walk.

PLATE 8. Colonna Gardens, Rome, alley and steps.

PLATE 9. Colonna Gardens, view across the flower-garden.

PLATE 10. Colonna Gardens, statuary.

PLATE 11. Villa d'Este, Tivoli, walk along the reservoirs.

PLATE 12. Villa Falconieri, Frascati, arched portico of the house.

PLATE 13. Villa Taverna, Frascati, rear façade and sunken courtyard entrance to the gardens.

PLATE 14. Villa Taverna, sunken courtyard between the house and gardens.

PLATE 15. Villa Taverna, central fountain and laurels.

PLATE 16. Villa Mondragone, Frascati, cypress-lined approach drive to the palace from the public road.

PLATE 17. Villa Mondragone, view from the terrace in front of the villa looking back toward Frascati and Rome.

PLATE 18. Villa Portici, Portici, pavilion.

PLATE 19. Villa Caprarola, Caprarola, casino from the entrance court.

PLATE 20. Villa Caprarola, circular courtyard of Palazzo Farnese.

166

INDEX

Text references are given first in roman type; illustrations follow in italic.